Land of Cotton, Land of Snow

by
Jan Chronister

ISBN: 978-1-886895-48-5

An imprint of Poetry Harbor

Cover photo by Jan Chronister

Copies of this chapbook are available at amazon.com or from the author at whispertreepress@gmail.com

CONTENTS

In the Night

After snowing all day
the plow roars by,
flashing lights reflect on bedroom walls,
scrape of blade on blacktop
dissolves into silence.

Down South
heavy fog
shrouds street lights,
christens neighborhoods
in orange mist.
1:30 a.m. train screams,
incessant whistle
a baby's cry.
It rumbles on,
leaves behind
empty hours.

Morning Rosary

I lie on my back
knees bent
hands on sides
palms down.

Imagine my navel
a bowl of water,
push it down
against the floor
while counting to ten,
then bring it up.

I arch my back
squeeze my buttocks
together.
Imagine
picking up a dime.
Instead I see
a string of beads,
envision each one
rising, then falling
as I raise and lower
my spine. Sometimes
a kink straightens
as the necklace
settles in place.

I never knew I'd spend
mornings like this,
looking at trees
upside down,
counting again and again,
seeking release.

Assurance

Spring unlocks
when I walk up the hill,
see frigid strip of lake.

I come down fast,
wind at my back.
Deer tracks alongside me
point the way,
indicate like math signs
that I am greater than
whatever lies ahead.

Absolution

On my knees
I crawl along our ditch,
pick out rocks thrown by a snowplow
or poured from sanders.
They nestle in dry grass
like Easter eggs,
some full size,
some pink quartz jelly beans.

Into the bucket I toss
chips of white limestone,
native gray basalt,
mica-flecked granite.
Each tells a long story.

This annual chore
cleanses me,
removes burdens
carried all winter.
I rake away dead grass—
green blades grow
into the clear air.

Daffodils

More April snow.
Kids on school bus
sing Christmas carols,
teenagers wear boots to prom.
Summer floats out of reach,
a distant dream.

Pale green spears
poke through cold,
remind us that soon
we will wake up to shouts
as yellow as the bus.

Green Melody

I hear music reach crescendo
when fiddleheads uncurl,
follow codes contained
in their DNA.

I don't understand
the science. I just know
my soul is fed
by the songs of plants.

Anticipation

I can't wait
until I walk
through tall flowers
that burn my legs
with summer heat,
rain black seeds
with every shake.

Coneflower, prairie clover,
black-eyed Susan—
seeds dormant all winter debut,
sing in colors so beautiful
they sting.

Heartsick

I sit at my desk,
open window sends
scent of lilies
my way, last grand
dames of summer.

On the front walk
too much perfume
follows me into the house
where vases hold fuchsia
explosions.

Every year
I revel in smells—
lilac, peony, marigold—
but only Stargazer's late August
sweetness chokes me
with tears.

Observations

In a distant field
I spot triangular specks
of wild turkeys.
Chives rebloom
after late summer rain,
marigolds rejoice.

On my bike ride
I notice a small blue spruce,
perfect for a Christmas tree.

Maybe I could dig it up,
take it south with us,
replant in red Georgia soil,
string white lights
to brighten long nights.

Broken Rib

Instructions from the ER
read "Take pain medication as ordered.
Don't drive, operate machinery,
climb ladders,
sign contracts,
go gambling,
participate in excessive shopping or spending."
I'd laugh if it didn't hurt so bad.

I rise slowly from bed,
chairs, toilet,
put the brakes on
my usual busy self,
miss a poetry event
I looked forward to
all summer.

I sit on the deck
in mid-October sun,
marvel at maple leaves
that glow from within.

There will be more summers,
more poems to read.
In time I'll be whole.

Flight Plan

In late October wind
maple's flame fades.
Each petiole breaks off,
leaves a scar.
Beneath the wound
plans are made
for spring blossoms,
helicopter seeds.

When my time comes
to let go, I hope
I've learned how
to grow wings and take off.

Out of Season

Snow slides off
still-green leaves
of lilacs and peonies.
Yesterday's robust
marigolds wear
stocking hats.

We saw the forecast,
figured fifty-percent chance
would happen somewhere else.

Two weeks before
the legendary blizzard of '91
we get a taste of what's ahead.

(The Halloween Blizzard of 1991 dumped over three
feet of snow and shut everything down for days.)

Parenting

There's something sad
about an empty nest
after fledglings graduate
to flight.

What was the site
of busy construction
now sits abandoned.
Where parents filled
stretched-out beaks,
only bits of shell,
whispers of down
remain.

Loosened by wind,
heavy with snow,
ragged bowls fall to earth.
I pick them up,
burn the brief history
of happiness.

Halloween

The day before we leave
I wake up to four inches of snow.

Everything I worried about,
fretted over being undone
erased by a fresh coverlet
patterned with golden leaves.

I open the door,
breathe in the smell of snow
before it's left behind.

Alabama

In front of mobile homes
on a country road,
men lean on pickups,
poke under hoods,
open mouths all
ask the same questions.

In Montgomery
rows of brick houses
once identical
now different,
some decorated,
some boarded up,
all faces Black.

Back on the highway
traces of cotton fluff
catch on roadside weeds.

Land of Cotton

South of Montgomery
we head into country
new to us.
Antebellum mansions
dominate small towns
skirted by worn wooden shacks
in places called
Three Notch
Cecil
Fitzpatrick.

Gentle hills disguise
a hard past
still alive in mothers' eyes
at the laundromat where we stop.

Three of every four washers
are out of order.
Same for dryers.
Empty vending machines,
peeling floor
says no one cares
how long people wait.

South Georgia, 1962–63

At a rally in Camilla
just down the road,
a pregnant Black woman,
kicked unconscious by police,
loses her baby.

Twenty miles north in Leesburg
Black teenage girls, some only 12,
attempt to integrate a theater,
are assaulted, arrested,
held forty-five days
in a squalid jail.

These stories
force me to face
the battles still being won
and lost.

Sunset

I drink in the western sky,
swallow, leave the moon
a milky crescent
at the bottom of my glass.

Solstice Fire

Friends up north report
celebrations have been cancelled
due to bad roads,
below zero temps.
I feel left out,
miss the heroics required
to make it though
a Wisconsin winter.

It's in the forties here,
overcast but not cold.
I sit on green grass,
burn brush, end up
with a pile of white coals
reminiscent of bones.

Under the Pecan Trees

Our house was built
in a pecan grove.
Every yard on the street
displays century-old giants
still dropping abundant nuts.

In December
the four behind our house
wave branches tipped with stars
exploding in warm sun.

I climb a ladder
to a wooden platform
that once held a child's slide,
gaze up as magic wands
transform me.

Farewell

Through bare branches of pecan trees,
opalesque full March moon
illuminates cascades of wisteria, azalea.
Tomorrow I return to a frozen landscape
shrouded in snow.

Snowbird

At our Wisconsin home
robins build a spring nest
on a downspout curve,
raise their chicks,
fly south in autumn.

On our Georgia lawn
dozens of russet breasts
reflect the winter sun—
not in a hurry,
not flustered by
home construction
or pulling up worms
for family food.

One day they leave,
cover the distance
in almost two weeks
that takes us three days.

I'm learning to fly
north to south
then reverse.
Plan what to take down,
what to bring back.

In dreams I become
a white bird
following the sun,
never sure if I'll return.

ACKNOWLEDGMENTS

Many thanks to the editors of the following publications where these poems have previously appeared, some in slightly different versions:

"Absolution." *The Thunderbird Review* (2023).

"Alabama." *Decennia,* Truth Serum Press (2019).

"Anticipation." *Echoes of the Wild*, Poetry for a Cause (2023).

"Assurance." *Bramble* (Summer 2023).

"Daffodils." *Your Daily Poem* Addendum (April 2023).

"Green Melody." *Echoes of the Wild*, Poetry for a Cause (2023.)

"Heartsick." *Heartsick* (2021).

"In the Night." *The Nemadji Review* (2023).

"Morning Rosary." *Last Stanza Poetry Journal*, Issue #14 (2023).

"Out of Season." *Duluth: Zenith City & Beyond*, Poetry Harbor (2023).

"Sunset." *Poetry Hall* Issue 19 (Spring 2023).

"Under the Pecan Trees." *Blue Heron Review* (Spring 2023).

ABOUT THE AUTHOR

Jan Chronister has been writing poetry for sixty years. Her work is widely published in state, regional, and national journals and anthologies. She has won awards from Lake Superior Writers, the TallGrass Writers Guild (Indiana), Highland Park Poetry (Illinois), the Emberlight Festival (Michigan), the Wisconsin Fellowship of Poets, and the League of Minnesota Poets.

Jan's first chapbook *Target Practice* was published by Parallel Press at the University of Wisconsin in 2009. *Casualties*, a chapbook of Holocaust poems, was published in 2017. Her first full-length collection *Caught between Coasts* was released by Clover Valley Press in 2018 and recognized as an Outstanding Book in Poetry by the Wisconsin Library Association (WLA.) A third chapbook, *Bird Religion*, came out in 2019 and was awarded an Honorable Mention in the Wisconsin Fellowship of Poets chapbook contest. A second full-length collection titled *Decennia* was published in 2020 by Truth Serum Press of Australia and received the Kops-Fetherling Award for Poetry.

Distanced: Poems from the Pandemic, Jan's fourth chapbook, was written to document the months of February through November 2020. It was recognized as an Outstanding Book in Poetry by the WLA. *Heartsick*, Jan's fifth chapbook, contains poems reflecting events in the poet's life from 2021. *Flight Patterns* (2022) was her sixth chapbook and third in an annual series. Jan also authored a chapbook about her father titled *Son of Norway*. A third full-length collection, *Duluth: Zenith City & Beyond*, was released in 2023.

Land of Cotton, Land of Snow is her fourth annual chapbook and recounts events and impressions from 2023.

Now retired from teaching English, Jan has turned her attention to her own writing as well as editing and publishing books for fellow poets. She splits her year between northern Wisconsin and South Georgia with her husband of fifty-plus years.

Made in the USA
Columbia, SC
30 November 2023

26937793R00019